Napoleon

Alexander Kennedy

Amazon.com/author/alexanderkennedy

Contents

Prologue

On the fateful day of 19 Brumaire—a month of the French Revolutionary calendar, soon to be abolished—the mood in the Council chambers was tense, even desperate. Three of the five Directors had resigned, and everyone knew the Directory wouldn't last much longer. Men in red togas huddled in the shadows, speaking in urgent whispers and casting around the sidelong glances of cornered thieves.

Headed by the fabulously corrupt Paul de Barras, the Directory Junta had overthrown Maximillien Robespierre's Reign of Terror in 1795, but proved no more popular with the French people than its predecessor. What success the Directory had enjoyed was mostly attributable to the brilliance of a single artillery officer, Napoleon Bonaparte. Bonaparte (who preferred before his coronation to be referred to by his last name, rather than his first) had masterminded an important victory in the early struggle around Toulon, and thereafter become a protégé of Barras. It was Barras, in fact, who had introduced him to Marie-Josèphe-Rose Tascher de la Pagerie, better known to history as Josephine. She was an unwanted mistress Barras was now looking to unload, and Bonaparte was more than willing to woo her in his patron's place, eventually marrying her. Perhaps in exchange for this favor, Bonaparte was placed in command of the Directory's Italian campaign.

But for the Directory, this relationship proved a Faustian bargain that destroyed them. Bonaparte had saved its rule from street protests in 1795 when he dispersed the Paris mobs with "a whiff of grapeshot"—in reality, a point-blank cannon barrage. As historian Paul Johnson observed, this marked a turning point in the Revolutionary years; not until 1830 did a popular uprising again determine the course of government, as "the era of the mob yielded to a new era of order under fear." Yet, though Bonaparte's victory over the mob preserved the Directory, every victory also increased his own reputation, making him a greater danger to them.

The same was true of his military campaigns in Italy and Egypt. Bonaparte battled the Austrian Habsburgs in a lightning campaign across Northern Italy, seizing and looting city after city of their riches, goods, and art. (He once said that he hoped to gather the treasures of all Europe in the Louvre, so that visitors could see them all in one place.) When he negotiated the Treaty of Campo Formio with Austria in 1797, making his gains official, he did not bother to consult the Directory before negotiating terms and establishing his new puppet states.

Almost any fool could see which way the wind was blowing, but not the fools of the Directory; they were too dependent on Bonaparte's reflected popularity to shore up their failing popularity at home. They financed another expedition, this time to Egypt to threaten Britain's colonial holdings.

Though this proved a military failure in most respects, the wonders of the exotic Near East entranced the French public, and Bonaparte's skilled propaganda made the expedition seem like yet another feather in his cap. Tipped off that the Directory's situation was rapidly deteriorating due to food shortages, runaway inflation, and endemic corruption, Bonaparte left his army and returned to France in haste. He arrived in the month of Brumaire.

Bonaparte quickly found three important backers for his intended coup. The first was the Abbé de Sièyes, whose pamphlet *What Is the Third Estate?* had been a key text of the original revolution, declaring the "third estate"—the lower orders—to be "everything" in the new nation, and the clergy and nobility to be only dead weight. But after years of turmoil, Sieyès saw the need for a stronger hand at the wheel, if for no other reason than to avoid a second bloody Terror.

Bonaparte's second important ally was Charles Maurice de Talleyrand-Périgord, a sly, skilled diplomat who survived from government to government over the succeeding decades, always ready to betray one patron to move on to the next. (At around this time, Talleyrand's demands of bribes from American officials led to the famous "XYZ Affair" of John Adams' presidency; Bonaparte later memorably described Talleyrand as "shit in a silk stocking.")

The third was Joseph Fouché, whose amorality and network of informants allowed him to adapt from regime to regime just as smoothly as Talleyrand. He later headed Napoleon's secret police, but for now, he fed the conspirators the inside information they needed to make their move.

Sieyès arranged a meeting for the two legislative houses of the Directory outside of Paris, where they would have no significant forces of their own to rally against Bonaparte's. Talleyrand was dispatched separately to buy Barras's resignation with a bribe of several million francs, but Barras agreed to resign before compensation was even mentioned, and so Talleyrand simply pocketed the bribe for himself.

But the "Five Hundred"—the lower house of the Directory—proved to have far more spine than Barras. Despite Bonaparte's surprise appearance at the head of a large group of grenadiers, the legislators began to heckle him as he tried to speak. Bonaparte's mere presence in the chamber was illegal, much less with an armed contingent. "The Constitution is dead" one yelled, and others shouted, "No dictators!", and yet another cried, "Kill, kill!" To Bonaparte's shock, the deputies began to physically assault him and his grenadiers, and having separated from his men when he tried to address the chamber, Bonaparte found himself surrounded by furious legislators, shaking him back and forth.

And then a very uncharacteristic thing happened: Bonaparte lost his nerve. The man who had—and later did again and again— coolly face personal peril and much larger enemy armies now found himself paralyzed and tongue-tied. The deputies continued to rally, led by the Jacobins—the faction once headed by Robespierre—but others of all stripes quickly joined the fight. The struggle was at a tipping point.

It was Napoleon's brother Lucien, the President of the Five Hundred, who carried the day in the end. As Bonaparte's grenadiers escorted him from the chambers, Lucien dropped his seal of office and slipped out to appeal to the Five Hundred's own Guardsmen outside. He told them that the deputies were rebels trying to assassinate France's most beloved general, the only man who could now preserve France's liberties. As his brother joined him, face bloody with scratches, Lucien drew his sword and pressed the point against Bonaparte's chest. The day that Napoleon Bonaparte did not respect French liberties, Lucien swore, he himself would run a sword through his brother's heart.

When that day arrived just a few years later, Lucien could not bring himself to fulfill his oath—he went into miserable, self-imposed exile instead—but at that moment, his melodramatic words carried the day, and changed history forever. The Guardsmen joined the grenadiers in storming the building to arrest the deputies. Seeing that their own guards had defected, the nerve of the deputies broke immediately, and the legislative chamber hosted a mad dash for the doors and windows. The ground outside was so thick with discarded red togas that it could be mistaken for a carpet.

Bonaparte, having recovered his usual self-possession, circulated a statement that he had been attacked by English spies among the deputies, but survived. Meanwhile, Lucien's troops combed the area around the meeting for the rest of the day. One deputy was yanked from a bush where he had been hiding; others were apprehended while drowning their sorrows at local inns and taverns. The captured deputies were escorted back and forced to formally dissolve the Directory, swearing loyalty instead to a new triumvirate government of Bonaparte, Sieyès , and Ducos.

Considering the bloodshed that had accompanied the overthrow of Louis XIV and the Reign of Terror that followed, the Brumaire Coup was remarkable for its bloodlessness. Bonaparte biographer Patrice Gueniffy noted that, for all Bonaparte's claims of near-assassination, the worst casualty of the day appears to be a grenadier who had his uniform's sleeve ripped in the scuffle. (Bonaparte claimed that the deputies had set on him with daggers, but if so, they must have been singularly unskilled at using them, for he was wholly unharmed.)

But it marked far more bloodshed to come, if not in the halls of power, than on the battlefields of Europe. Talleyrand understood that the future of Europe lay in stability and the appropriate balance of power, but Bonaparte, for all his modernity, was much like his Bourbon predecessors in seeking *gloire*—the honor of military conquest—above any other goal. No man was better suited to pursue it. His loss of nerve during the coup—one of the few lapses in his brilliant career—was not soon repeated, and having secured power at home, Bonaparte could unleash both his modernizing genius and his dictatorial impulses upon the rest of Europe. His quest soon upended the established order and made him the master of a continent, briefly including even Spain, and much of Russia.

The French revolutionaries called the year of the coup "Year VII," but the rest of the world called it 1799—the year that Napoleon came to power.

Introduction

"History is the version of past events that people have decided to agree upon."

—Napoleon Bonaparte

Great military minds hold a special place in history. From Marius of Rome to General Patton, historians have always examined the men who led others into battle, and few of these are remembered as clearly as Napoleon Bonaparte. Napoleon's military successes were nearly always against numerically superior forces, but his brilliant tactics, from picking favorable terrain to luring his enemies into clever traps usually led him to victory. Never before in history had armies of such size clashed on an open battlefield, and these conflicts are still studied in military academies today.

But it is not just his tactics that led to his success. Napoleon managed to secure the love and respect of his people, through brilliant social reforms, community projects, and the clever use of propaganda. Much like Julius Caesar, Bonaparte understood that a well-spoken message was every bit as important as victory on the battlefield.

Yet that is not why Napoleon's life is significant or interesting. The truth is that he was born into a little-known family, with hardly anything but a relatively common title to his name. In a time when parentage and ancestry typically determined the trajectory of someone's life, Napoleon rose from obscurity to Emperor before he was thirty years old, a feat unmatched by any except Alexander the Great—and even Alexander had the legacy of a father upon which to build.

Napoleon's life and career was tumultuous, yet filled with far more victories than losses. At the height of his power and popularity, it took the combined strength of all of Europe to stop him—and even that had to be done twice before he was exiled for good.

But Napoleon is still not forgotten, even two centuries after his death. His legacy remains, from the current European legal system that he instituted to the everyday fact that traffic sticks to the right side of the road. A story of obscurity to Emperor, Napoleon's life remains one of the most fascinating narratives in modern history.

Chapter 1:
Early Life

"There is no such thing as 'accident;' it is fate misnamed."

—**Napoleon Bonaparte**

Born Into War

Musket shots rang out in the pine forest. A ragged collection of farmers, peasants, and poor noblemen scurried up a harsh incline of granite, thick with trees and brush. French infantry chased these rebels into the mountains of Corsica. A few of them took aim, leaning against the pines, careful to make each shot count. They didn't have many musket balls left, and it was difficult to find more.

The movement for Corsican independence was in shambles. Patriots had fled to the mountains at the center of the island in a last-ditch effort to combat the 30,000 French troops that had landed on their shores. For centuries, the island's poor inhabitants had undergone extreme exploitation and colonization by the Romans, Moors, and most recently the Genoese. After four decades of fighting with the Republic of Genoa and the Genoese defeat in the Seven Years' War, they had decided to sell Corsica to the French to pay their war debt and to rid themselves of the stubborn island.

In the spring of 1769, the French were keen to squash any thought of independence and secure the island as a military outpost in the Mediterranean. France was the most advanced civilization in Europe, and the unorganized and ill-equipped rebels didn't stand a chance.

Among the rebels was a twenty-three year old student named Carlo Maria di Bonaparte, and his wife Letizia. Carlo was a Corsican patriot who worked closely with the leader of the Corsican independence movement, Pasquale Paoli. When the French began to seize the island, Carlo, Letizia, and their newborn son Giuseppe fled from their home in the Corsican capitol of Ajaccio with Paoli and his other supporters.

The rebels continued fighting for another year with thousands killed before they finally were defeated by the French, but Letizia was pregnant and Carlo had to consider the future of his family. He decided to capitulate to the new French authority and return to his ancestral home in Ajaccio. In August of 1769, Letizia went into labor while at Mass celebrating the Feast of Assumption. She was rushed back to the family home and gave birth to another son. They named him Napoleone di Buonaparte.

"I was born when Corsica was perishing," Napoleon later wrote. "Thirty-thousand French poured onto our shores, drowning the throne of liberty in waves of blood. The cries of the dying, the drones of the oppressed, and the tears of despair surrounded my cradle from the moment of my birth."

Napoleon spent his childhood hating France. He resented his father for submitting to French rule, but Carlo believed that France might offer the family access to higher status. Carlo later traveled to Paris as a representative of the Corsican parliament. There he wondered at the immensity and splendor of Versailles, and hoped that his children might one day reach such a level of nobility.

A Military Education

The Bonapartes descended from minor Tuscan nobility who came to Corsica in the 16th century seeking a better life. They had a title, a country home, and a home in the city, but they were still considered poor. Under French rule, nobility without money had an opportunity to send their children to schools in France on a scholarship. While in Paris, Carlo was granted a scholarship for Napoleon to attend a military academy at Brienne-le-Chateau.

Napoleon was raised by his mother until he traveled to France to begin his military education in 1779. His father was a lawyer and was elected to the Corsican Assembly. He spent little time with the children. Letizia was pregnant thirteen times and gave birth to eight surviving children. Napoleon later said all of his success was due to the training his mother gave him.

At the age of ten, Napoleon journeyed to France to begin his schooling. He did not speak French, and the other children were prone to teasing him as an outsider. He became a loner with few friends. He threw himself into his studies, and read endlessly about history, geography, philosophy, and great military leaders. He eventually learned to speak French, but for his entire life spoke with a heavy Corsican accent. He was a proud and, at times, stubborn student, but he received good marks in most of his classes.

At fifteen, he was promoted to The Royal Military Academy (the elite Ecole Militarie) in Paris, a finishing school for young officers-to-be. He continued to excel in the subjects he was interested in, like geography and math, but did poorly in German. One of his professors wrote of him, "He would go far in favorable conditions." He continued to identify as a Corsican, despite his growing assimilation into French society. He yearned for a day when he might return to Corsica and join the struggle for its independence. At the Royal Academy, he grew to resent the French for their snobbery and decadence. Officers at the academy were mostly sons of French aristocracy, and they were treated as such.

When Napoleon graduated in September of 1785, he began his apprenticeship with an artillery regiment. Other graduating officers from higher nobility were offered the best positions in the cavalry or infantry, but since Napoleon came from a poorer background, he was selected for a position with the less desirable artillery. He was well suited for the post, however, because of his skills in mathematics and his ability to sight the guns. At this time, France had developed better artillery technology, which made the cannon a more essential part of the military.

Revolution in the Air

France was about to undergo drastic changes. When Carlo traveled to Paris, he was unaware that there were already whispers of rebellion against the King. King Louis XVI had run up the nation's debt supporting the American Revolution, and the Queen—Marie Antoinette—had a penchant for spending on fashion and gambling, all on the French tax payers' dime.

Napoleon served as a second lieutenant in La Fere artillery regiment in Valence and then Auxonne. He was extremely bored during this time. He had high hopes for his military career, but he didn't see how there would ever be an opportunity to rise in rank. He dreamed of becoming a famous author, and even wrote a history of Corsica, and tried to write a novel. He believed he was destined for greatness, but his position in the rigid French society did not allow him a chance to prove himself on the basis of merit. He was miserable and depressed, and instead focused on his studies. He wrote, "I come home to dream by myself, and to give myself over to all the forces of my melancholy. What fury drives me to wish for my own destruction? No doubt because I see no place for myself in this world."

Then, on July 14th 1789, Paris erupted in revolution. Crowds shouted the revolutionary motto of "liberty, equality, and brotherhood." Napoleon had traveled back to Corsica before the outbreak of revolution. He spent the next two years entrenched in a heated conflict between Corsican nationalists, revolutionaries, and royalists.

The revolution in France had opened the door of opportunity for Napoleon, however. The new National Assembly was challenging the authority of the king, and dismantling the privileges of the clergy and the nobility. Many aristocratic officers were fleeing the country, and an opportunity had arisen for the quick promotion of skilled officers. Napoleon welcomed the revolution. He believed it might abolish the sort of discrimination he had endured as a child.

In Corsica, Napoleon aligned himself with a Jacobin faction, and raised a battalion of volunteers on the island. The Jacobins led the revolution in France, and Napoleon saw this as a shrewd political move. He had dreamed of becoming a leader in Corsica alongside Pasquale Paoli, but had come to believe that the ideals of the revolution were more important than Corsican independence, and thought that Corsica should now accept French rule under the new government. His allegiance to the Revolution eventually came into conflict with Paoli's nationalism, and the two factions, along with their supporters, clashed with each other on the island until Paoli eventually defeated Napoleon. He and the entire Bonaparte family were forced to leave Corsica. Napoleon never returned.

In Paris the mobs stormed the Tulleries Palace, and forced the king to wear the revolutionary bonnet. In the summer of 1792, Bonaparte was on leave in Paris to witness the fall of the French monarchy. In August, the mob killed the king's Swiss Guard. A few days later, the king was dethroned and imprisoned with the rest of the royal family in the tower of the Temple. In January of the following year, the king was executed by guillotine.

With his defeat in Corsica behind him and his ideals shaken by the split with Paoli, Napoleon set his sights back on France. He wrote to his brother, "Among so many conflicting ideas the honest man is confused and distressed. Since one must choose sides, one might as well choose the side which is victorious. Considering the alternative, it is better to eat, than to be eaten." He decided he wanted to be French, and to join in the spirit of the revolution.

In June of 1793, he returned to France to find chaos. The king and queen had been executed, and Maximilien Robespierre was now the leader of the Republic. The revolution then became "the terror." Robespierre executed anyone who spoke against the ideals of the revolution, including fellow Jacobins who disagreed with his dictatorial leadership. A civil war had begun in France, and other European monarchs, alarmed by the destruction of the monarchy, and fearful of the spread of the revolution, had begun amassing troops along France's borders to intervene in the conflict.

Toulon

Napoleon had been promoted to the rank of Captain in 1792, despite the lengthy absence from his regiment while he was fighting in Corsica. A pro-republican pamphlet which Napoleon had written in 1793 gave him the support of Augustin Robespierre, the younger brother of Maximilien. With his favor and the help of a fellow Corsican, Napoleon was given command of Republican forces assigned to the Siege of Toulon. Pro-royalists in the city had captured the heights where the cannon were located with the support of a British fleet that was defending the city from the harbor.

Napoleon invented a plan to capture the heights and bombard the British ships to drive them out of the harbor. Aristocratic generals were still fleeing the country, and Napoleon saw this mission as an opportunity for quick promotion. Napoleon led the charge on the heights himself, and was wounded by a bayonet in the thigh. His men took the heights, however, and destroyed ten British ships in the process. After the battle, he was promoted to Brigadier General.

The Terror

In Paris there was chaos. Robespierre used the guillotine to maintain unity and order. He said, "Liberty cannot be maintained unless criminals lose their heads." Unfortunately, Robespierre began to turn on his fellow Jacobins, calling them traitors to the revolution, drawing up false charges against them, and eventually executing fellow leaders of the revolution he saw as threats. Napoleon hated the terror, but he hated chaos more. He believed, at this time, that in order for general liberty to be maintained, some individual liberty must be given up, an idea closely aligned with that of Robespierre. But Robespierre had gone too far. His reign of terror was over. In December 1794, his government was overthrown, and he was sent to the guillotine as well.

Chapter 2:

Making His Mark

"Four hostile newspapers are more to be feared than a thousand bayonets."

—**Napoleon Bonaparte**

13 Vendermiaire

In the spring of 1795, Napoleon headed for Paris. His victory in Toulon gave him the promotion he desired, but he was determined to rise even higher. In Paris, he attended the salons patronized by the aristocratic women. He was seen as just another ambitious young soldier—not wealthy, and not even really French. Most women who saw him at this time described him as repulsive and wanted nothing to do with him. After several months in Paris, but nothing to show for it, Napoleon thought he might have reached another dead end. Fortunately for him, however, he was in exactly the right place at exactly the right time.

On October 5th, 1795, a group of royalists supported by national guardsmen rebelled against the current government, the National Convention, with the goal of restoring the monarchy. Paul Barras, one of the leaders of the new government knew of Napoleon's success in Toulon. He called upon Napoleon to defend the Convention in the Tuileries Palace. Napoleon remembered how the mob had massacred the king's Swiss Guard just three years prior, and he was determined that such an event would not be repeated. He ordered a young cavalry officer named Joachim Murat to secure the large cannon at the Palace, which Napoleon then used against the mob. Fourteen-hundred royalists were killed, and the National Convention was saved.

When the French Revolution began, revolutionary France wanted to distinguish itself from the France of the past. One of the ways chosen to accomplish this was the creation of a new calendar. This new calendar started the year the revolution began. "13 Vendermiaire" refers to the 5th of October on the revolutionary calendar, and is considered by some to be the day the French Revolution ended.

Napoleon was heralded as a great hero for his actions that day. He had used every weapon at his disposal. No one had used cannon on a Paris mob before, but Napoleon justified his actions, saying, "The enemy attacked us. We killed a great many of them. I could not be happier." He had shown that he was more concerned with order than liberty, and in the process he was seen as a defender of the Republic and a national hero. It was later said by the Scottish philosopher Thomas Carlyle that the Revolution ended with a "Whiff of grapeshot" from Napoleon's cannon. Within three weeks, Napoleon was promoted to full general. He was now commander of the Army of the Interior and The Army of Italy.

Josephine de Beauharnais

Josephine de Beauharnais was romantically involved with Paul Barras, a key figure in the overthrow of Robespierre, a leader in the National Convention, and a leader in the new government, which came to be known as The Directory. When Napoleon met Josephine, she was living in a house Barras provided for her. Impressed, by the amount of influence Josephine has within the elite circles of French society, he was spellbound, and quickly fell in love.

Josephine had two young children. She was a Creole aristocrat from Martinique who had come to Paris in an attempt to support herself after her husband had died. She had affairs with members of the high society, and used these connections to gain financial security. Napoleon thought she could help him with his ambitions, but he was also madly in love with her.

Unfortunately for him, she found Napoleon repugnant. She overcame these feelings to please him, but she did not return his love. However, she was growing older, and her beauty was beginning to fade. Napoleon didn't seem concerned, and Josephine knew she needed a protector. On March 9, 1796, they married. With Barras's help, Napoleon received command of The Army of Italy, and two days after the marriage he was in Italy on the offensive.

First Italian Campaign

Napoleon had never commanded an army before. Just 27 years old when he arrived in Italy to command the army, he had been promoted above more experienced generals. His officers in Italy knew he'd been promoted because of his connections in Paris, and Paris didn't expect anything from him. Napoleon, of course, had other ideas.

"Soldiers, you are naked and ill fed," Napoleon declared to his soldiers upon his arrival in Italy. For almost two years, the Army of Italy had stagnated in the foothills of the Italian Alps under incompetent commanders. When Napoleon arrived, the officers and the men quickly realized he was a serious leader who meant business.

"I will lead you into the most fertile plains in the world," Napoleon said to his troops. "Rich provinces and great cities will lie in your power. You will find there honor, glory, and riches.

Napoleon had an excellent ability to motivate his troops. Like an accomplished actor, he could portray any emotion, and evoke any desired reaction from his audience in return. The soldiers were enthralled by him, and he inspired them to follow him into battle. After getting his troops into fighting shape, he led them on an offensive against the forces of Piedmont, hoping to defeat the weaker Piedmontese before they can link up with the Austrians. On April 2, 1796, Bonaparte led his army forward.

Napoleon had 38,000 troops; the Austrians had 38,000, and the Piedmontese had 25,000. Napoleon used a tactic that eventually became common for him. He marched quickly toward the Piedmontese position, and in two weeks he won six battles and destroyed the Piedmont army.

A Piedmontese officer said, "They sent a young madman who attacks left, right and from the rear. It is an intolerable way of making war." On April 26, Peidmont surrendered. By attacking one of the allied armies and overwhelming it with superior force, Napoleon was able to isolate each army and destroy each individually. In later campaigns, he used this exact tactic often, to great success.

After knocking Piedmont out of the war, Napoleon focused the French effort on the Austrians in the Northwest of Italy. This part of the campaign was marked by the Siege of Mantua, where the Austrians held a large garrison. The siege lasted for a year, during which the French put down four attempts by the Austrians to relieve the garrison. He had victories at the battles of Castiglione, Bassano, Arcole, and Rivoli.

In the meantime, Napoleon had demanded gold and silver after his victory over Piedmont, and he used this to pay his troops. Morale was high, and Napoleon used this momentum to his advantage as he began chasing the Austrians out of Italy.

The Austrians attempted to make a stand at Lodi, where a river separated the Austrian position from the French. The only way across the river was over a narrow bridge. Napoleon worked his men into a passionate fervor and astonished the Austrians by ordering a frontal assault on the bridge. The French troops bravely crossed into a hail of enemy fire. They come across so quickly and threw themselves into the battle so selflessly that the Austrians were surprised and quickly began to pull out of the city. During the battle, Napoleon was seen aiming and firing the cannon himself, which earned him the respect of his men—and the nickname "Little Corporal."

After the battle of Rivoli where the Austrians lost 14,000 men, their position in Italy was broken. Napoleon had defeated the Austrians in Italy, and soon he would make a turn toward Vienna. In less than a year, despite low expectations, he had conquered Italy for France. He finally had evidence of his greatness, and came to believe that he was destined to accomplish even more. He told an aide, "In our time no one has the slightest conception of what is great. It is up to me to give them an example." After leading his army into Milan on May 5, 1796, he wrote, "From that moment I foresaw what I might be. Already I saw the earth float from beneath me, as if I were being carried into the sky."

In Milan he was greeted as a liberator by the Italians from their Austrian rulers. "We come to break your chains," he said, "Our only quarrel is with the tyrants who have enslaved you." He made himself the head of a provisional Italian government, began to spread the ideal of the revolution in Italy, and, while they weren't looking, began to loot the country of its gold and art.

Josephine the Unfaithful

Napoleon wanted Josephine to join him in Italy, but she did not want to leave Paris. Hers was a life of luxury and parties, and she enjoyed the company of a young, seductive officer in Napoleon's absence. Napoleon sent her letter after letter pleading with her to join him in Italy, but she was afraid she would be bored in Italy, and despite their marriage, she was not in love with him.

Finally, Josephine gave in to Napoleon's requests. One of her friends said, "She wept as if she was going to a torture chamber." Upon Josephine's arrival in Milan, Napoleon greeted her with a palace full of flowers. They spent their third night together as a married couple in Milan. Two days later, Napoleon left to continue his campaign against the Austrians.

Victory and Propaganda

During Napoleon's campaign in Italy, he founded two newspapers. One was distributed to his troops and the other was circulated in France. Napoleon understood that victory in battle was only one element of his success. In order to rise to even greater heights, he needed to control information, particularly about his own persona. His papers spoke highly of the successes of the young general, and omitted his failures. Because of this, his image was transformed into something legendary.

In addition, his confiscation of precious metals, jewels and more than three hundred paintings and sculptures added to his glory in the eyes of the French people, and also went to pay the long-standing debt the French government had accumulated after years of war. As he moved farther into Europe, he began to commission works of art that romantically portrayed his victories and added to his allure. In this respect, Napoleon was well ahead of his time. He was able to utilize the cheaper mass printing technology available to publicize his achievements and thrust himself into the political sphere of France.

Chasing Austrians

During his reign over Italy, Napoleon continued to make war with the Austrians. In Italy, his proclamation of the ideals of the French Revolution had not placated the Italians, who now saw their country looted of its treasures. The people began to doubt Napoleon's image as a liberator. The general met any Italian rebellion with extreme force, ordering rebels shot and towns burned.

Just two weeks after his victory in Rivoli, Napoleon had chased the Austrians over the Alps. By April 7, 1797, he was only 75 miles from Vienna. Astounded by the speed and success of the advancing French troops, and after another loss at the Battle of Tarvis, the Austrians sued for peace. Napoleon himself negotiated with the Austrian diplomats, a fact that worried the weak new government in France, which already feared a coup d'état. Napoleon's military success and his propaganda campaign had already made him a popular figure in France, and The Directory worried he might attempt to challenge their power.

During his negotiation with the Austrians, Napoleon demanded Belgium, the west bank of the Rhine, and control of most of Northern

Italy. The Austrians objected to Napoleons demands, and the general, who was said to be prone to bouts of rage, flung over a tea service and shocked the Austrian delegation with his fury. Pointing to the broken porcelain, he exclaimed, "This is what will happen to your empire. Your empire is nothing but an old maid servant accustomed to being raped by everyone!" Bonaparte behaved like a madman, the Austrian diplomats reported, but he got what he wanted.

For the first time, Napoleon saw that his skills were not limited to the battlefield. He had also proven himself a statesman, and he returned to Paris at the end of 1797 with a peace treaty in hand. He was 28. In one and a half years, he had taken a demoralized Army of Italy to victory over the Austrians and brought peace to the continent of Europe. France was still at war with Great Britain, but a peace, though fragile, had been won by Napoleon, and France praised him for it.

A Hero for France

France needed a hero. The public viewed Napoleon as a possible answer to the political chaos that had plagued France since the beginning of the revolution. One government after another had risen and fallen under weak leadership, but Napoleon had brought a tenuous peace to Europe in short order, and had proven his ability as a military leader and a statesman. The current government, The Directory, was fragile, and the French economy remained weak, which only added to public skepticism of the incumbent leadership.

The public turned to Napoleon and waited for his next move. He had already begun planning a proposed invasion of the British Isles while he was still in Italy, but the task of organizing such a campaign remained daunting. The Directory was fearful of a potential challenge, but he was still waiting for an opportune moment to seize power. He told an aide, "Everything I have done up until now is nothing. I am only at the beginning of the course I must run. I can no longer obey. I have tasted command, and I cannot give it up."

The French government came upon a solution to their problem with Napoleon's rise in stature. They were ill-prepared to invade Britain, but they could use Napoleon to disrupt British trade in an attempt to weaken the British Empire. They decided to send him to Egypt, which was at that time under the control of the Ottoman Empire, but remained an important link in the British trade route to India. In Egypt, Napoleon would find new glory.

The Campaign in Egypt

In 1789, Egypt was a strange and alien land to Europeans. The Pyramids, the Sphinx, and the distant wonders of an ancient land not yet explored by modern Europeans enchanted the imaginations of the French. Napoleon brought 167 scientists, mathematicians, naturalists, and geographers with him on his expedition—along with 35,000 troops. After eluding the British fleet in the Mediterranean, Napoleon landed in Alexandria on July 1, 1798, and quickly captured the city. On July 3, he led his troops across the desert into Cairo.

Egypt was a wondrous country for Napoleon. Later paintings portrayed his visit to the Sphinx, still buried up to its neck in desert sand. The diverse culture of Egyptians, Syrians, Turks, and others interested him.

But control of Egypt seemed impossible. Military experts of the period believed that a European army could never conquer the Middle East. Egypt was controlled by a military faction of the Ottoman Empire called the Mamluks, who were known as the fiercest warriors in the region.

Napoleon fought the Mamluks at the Battle of Surbra Khit and again at the Battle of the Pyramids. The Mamluks were primarily made up of mounted cavalry, and used swords as opposed to the French muskets. Napoleon was able to defeat the Mamluks by forming his troops into defensive squares, with one row of men kneeling and a second row standing. The fearless Mamluks charged the French cannons and defensive positions, but they were no match for the superior weaponry of the French army. Their cavalry became trapped in the crossfire between the squares and the French made short order of them. Twenty-nine French casualties were reported, while 2,000 Mamluks were killed.

Not only was French troop morale boosted, but the victory also shook the foundations of power in the entire region. The Ottomans suddenly realized that their weapons and tactics had become severely outdated, and Europe realized that incursion and conquest in the East might be more feasible than previously believed.

As Napoleon moved further into Egypt, the fleets of French ships defending the harbor in Alexandria was surprised by the sudden appearance of the British Royal Navy.

Admiral Horatio Nelson, whom Napoleon had slipped past in the Mediterranean, suspected the French fleet had gone to Egypt. He set a course for Alexandria, and on August 1 arrived, to the despair of the French. The ensuing naval engagement became known as the Battle of the Nile. Fifteen Royal Navy ships of the line met seventeen French ships in one of the most decisive naval victories of the period.

Admiral Nelson's ships attacked the French fleet which had anchored in a firing line defending the harbor. Nelson, utilizing the tactics that became the standard for naval engagements for the following century, split his ships, cutting across the front of the leading French ship. Half of his ships faced the French from the shore, and the other from the sea. Caught in the crossfire, the French stood little chance. The battle lasted for three days, and resulted in thousands of French wounded and killed and thousands more captured. The British fleet ultimately destroyed all but two of the French ships. Napoleon and his 35,000 troops ashore in Egypt were trapped.

In early 1799, Napoleon led part of his army into Syria. He assaulted his way up the coast, attacking Arish, Gaza, Jaffa, and Haifa. In Jaffa, he met strong resistance during an assault on the garrison, the first of many setbacks. The Sultan of Turkey declared war on the French, Napoleon had been unable to destroy the fortress at Acre, and his troops became sick with and outbreak of Bubonic Plague. He retreated back to Cairo. Without supplies or means of escape, he was forced to live among the Egyptians and his soldiers had to loot and steal to survive.

At the beginning of the Egyptian Campaign, Napoleon had seen his glory reach new heights. He said, "I was full of dreams. I saw myself founding a new religion, marching into Asia, riding an elephant, a turban on my head, and in my hand the new Koran." After the loss of his fleet and mounting setbacks, morale was low.

Despite the military failure in Egypt, the expedition was not for nothing. The scientists that joined in Napoleon's conquest spent their time in Egypt compiling a comprehensive history of the country called Description of Egypt, a 24-volume work. Scientists had discovered new species of plants and animals, measured the dimensions of the Pyramids and the Sphinx, and most importantly they had discovered the Rosetta Stone. This slab of granite was engraved with writing in three ancient languages, and became the key to decipher ancient Egyptian hieroglyphics.

Chapter 3:

Seizing Power

"In order to govern, the question is not to follow out a more or less valid theory, but to build with whatever materials are at hand."
—Napoleon Bonaparte

Positioned for Power

Napoleon saw an opportunity. On August 23, 1799, he secretly set sail for France, leaving more than 30,000 French troops abandoned in Egypt. Napoleon gave them a simple message: "Extraordinary circumstance alone have persuaded me to pass through enemy lines and return to Europe."

During his time in Egypt, Austria and Russia had declared war on France. The Directory, still floundering for popular support, couldn't balance its budget, and a civil war raged in the country.

Napoleon decided that his moment had come. When he landed on the continent on October 9, 1799, he was greeted by cheering crowds. The military campaign in Egypt had been a disaster, but his propaganda had been victorious. He appeared to the people to be a great conqueror of distant lands. They believe he was destined for greatness, as he himself believed. When he arrived, he was seen as a savior come to rescue the French people. By October 16, he was in Paris preparing to maneuver for power.

Josephine's Infidelity

While Napoleon was trapped in Egypt, Josephine had bought a house six miles from Paris. It was called Malmaison, and included 300 acres of gardens, fountains, and woods. While waiting for Napoleon to return, she had continued to entertain her young lover. Napoleon finally discovered the affair when an aide told him the truth. He was destroyed when he learned of her infidelity and, in another fit of rage, he took the wife of an officer as his mistress. He wrote to his brother, "The veil is torn. I am tired of grandeur. All my feelings have dried up. I no longer care about my glory. At 29 I have exhausted everything."

When Napoleon retuned to Paris, he intended to divorce Josephine, but after his popular exploits in Egypt and his rise to fame and power, Josephine suddenly became fearful she might lose her status if she were to lose Napoleon. When he arrived, at Malmaison he locked himself in his room and refused to see Josephine. For an entire night she begged him to take her back, pounding on his door and sobbing. At first Napoleon refused to hear it, but by the morning he had weakened and decided to take her back. Josephine never took another lover again, while Napoleon, despite claiming to love her best, did what pleased him with his mistresses.

The Coup

Napoleon hadn't been in France more than a week when it became clear that the time had come to try for power. The Directory was about to be demolished. The war debt was mounting, thieves roamed the countryside, and draft evasion was at an all-time high. The Directory appeared powerless, and whispers of an impending coup spread through the halls of government. Napoleon wanted to take power for himself, but he needed a plan. He allied himself with a band of conspirators, including his brother Lucien, who was elected president of the lower house on the basis of Napoleon's popularity. They were joined by Emmanuel Sieyes, one of the Directors. The politicians who intended to take power needed the support of Napoleon, and did not suspect that he intended to take power for himself.

It was supposed to be a parliamentary coup, not a military coup. Bonaparte was only to be called upon to restore order if the need arose. On November 9, 1799, Bonaparte and Sieyes put their plan into motion. The plan was to vote in a provisional government and draft a new constitution. None of the plotters believed any violence would be necessary. Bonaparte and Sieyes wanted the parliament to vote them into power, thereby giving the coup a semblance of legitimacy.

Lucien was supposed to convince the lower house to abolish the government and vote in new leadership, but he was unable to have his way. The parliament began to put up resistance. Opposition to the abolition of the government won favor with most of the assembly, and they insisted on a renewal of each deputy's oath to the existing constitution.

This took hours to complete. Meanwhile, Napoleon waited outside the assembly hall in the wings, growing impatient. Eventually, Napoleon could not wait any longer. He stormed into the legislative house (an illegal action by a military officer), followed by his Grenadiers. The house erupted into chaos. The members of the assembly saw the soldiers marching into the parliament and believed it was a military coup, assuming (rightly) that Napoleon intended to take over the government. Any further attempt to shroud the intentions of Napoleon and his cohorts seemed impossible, but Lucien stepped in to reassure the members. The assembly still wanted Napoleon thrown out, and he was escorted out.

The coup seemed to have misfired. Lucien realized that the opening for action was rapidly closing. He drew his sword and approached Napoleon, proclaiming, "Believe me soldiers of France, if Napoleon aspires to take over the government of France, to become dictator, I'd run him through." Suddenly, the soldiers stormed the legislative hall. The legislators, fearing for their lives, scrambled to escape, some even hurriedly flinging themselves out the windows.

The political coup became a military coup, and by two o' clock that morning a small band of the insurgent leaders met to vote on the provisional government. It was to be a tripartite consul with Napoleon as one of the three consuls. Though he initially had to share power with Sieyes and the other consul, within a week Napoleon rewrote the constitution again and made himself the head of state. He assumed the title of First Consul.

The Revolution is Over

"The Revolution is over," Napoleon said, then added, "I am the revolution." It was the beginning of the new century, the year 1800, Napoleon was just 30 years old, and as First Consul he was the most powerful man in France. With Napoleon firmly in control of the government, the French Revolution had come to an end. For over a decade the country had suffered at the hands of mostly incompetent governments who had failed to restart the economy or pay off debts. France had survived the revolution and the terror, and it craved a leader who would preserve the ideals of the revolution and also take the country into greatness. Napoleon fit this role perfectly.

The Second Italian Campaign

The war in Italy, the campaign in Egypt, and, of course, the cleverly positioned propaganda that advertised these exploits back in France propelled Napoleon to fame, and helped to confirm his takeover through the support of the people. But war also became a way for Napoleon to maintain his popular support after he had secured the position of First Consul. France was still at war with Great Britain and Austria, and in the spring of 1800 Napoleon led a daring mission to surprise the Austrians in Italy again. He took 40,000 men across the icy St. Bernard's Pass in the Alps. They dragged artillery on pine trees and supplies in canoes through the snow over the mountains at an altitude of 10,500 feet. It was a military maneuver that had not been attempted since 218 BC, when the Carthaginian general Hannibal crossed the

Alps to attack the Romans. Napoleon was doubtlessly aware of this symmetry.

On May 20, Napoleon crossed the Alps himself. Napoleon's crossing was later romanticized in a portrait of the general riding a bucking white horse, but he actually rode on the back of steady mule. The crossing was difficult, with Napoleon nearly falling off the side of a cliff on at least one occasion, but he and his troops successfully entered Northern Italy in just six days. On June 14, after several days searching for the enemy, they met the Austrians at Marengo, 45 miles from Milan.

The Austrians led by General Melas outnumbered the French, and led an attack that nearly broke the French lines. Napoleon led a tactical retreat that convinced Melas he had been victorious, but Napoleon never stopped riding his lines and encouraging his men. Late in the day, after Melas had left command of the battle to his subordinates, Napoleon led a devastating artillery barrage and cavalry charge that broke the Austrian Army. By the end of the day, the French had lost 6,000 men, while the Austrians had lost 14,000. It was a decisive victory for Napoleon, and almost immediately led to the Austrians abandoning their position in Italy. In his first Italian campaign it had taken Napoleon a year to drive the Austrians out of Italy. Because of his daring decision to cross the Alps and attack the Austrians from the north, it took Napoleon less than a month to do the same the second time.

The next year, the Emperor of Austria sued for peace. A peace treaty was again signed with the Austrians, and the British followed soon after. For the first time in ten years, everyone in Europe was at peace, though the treaty with the British was quite fragile. The French had witnessed many leaders and governments come and go in the revolutionary years. If they had been skeptical of their new leader before, his victory over Austria and his peace with the British suggested that Napoleon might indeed be the strong leader they had hoped for. Napoleon was aware of this dynamic as well, saying, "My power depends on my glory, and my glory on my victories." The people of France recognized that Napoleon might be a successful leader, and he quickly moved to consolidate his power.

Dictator for Life

Napoleon signed the Treaty of Amiens with the British in March of 1802 after forcing the Austrians to agree to peace the year before. The Revolutionary Wars were over, and a new era had begun for France. With his popularity soaring, Napoleon amended the constitution to give himself near dictatorial powers. He received overwhelming popular support in a vote to confirm the new document. Napoleon used the tenuous peace in Europe to focus his attention on France's colonies, many of which had become nearly autonomous during the chaotic Revolutionary years. Attempts to regain control of defiant colonies in the Caribbean largely failed, however, and in 1803, Napoleon sold the Louisiana Territory to the United States for just three cents an acre to aid the floundering economy.

The peace with the British was weak, and it was unclear how long it would last. The British contested Napoleon's annexation of Piedmont and did not remove their troops in Malta. By May of 1803, Great Britain had declared war on France again. Napoleon moved to reassemble his invasion force in Boulogne, again considering the possibility of a ground invasion on the British Isles.

Napoleon secured power incrementally. Each victory, both military and domestic, resulted in a slight increase in his power. He set out to prove he could govern as well as he could fight, and used his popular support to institute sweeping reforms that laid the foundation of modern France. He built parks, roads, schools, and canals, all public works that contributed to his popularity, contribute to job growth and the restoration of the economy, and, of course, entrench his legacy. "I will make Paris the loveliest city there ever was or ever could be," he said, "and France the greatest country on earth."

His new government was highly centralized, with a tightly structured and expansive bureaucracy. Several assassination attempts attributed to Jacobins and Bourbon royalists enabled Napoleon to consolidate his power further on the grounds that the country was under threat of a return to monarchist rule. He produced a government modeled on the Roman Empire, where Napoleon's rule was enshrined in the constitution as a matter of familial legacy, as he believed this would make a royalist takeover more unlikely.

Creating Modern French Society

Many of Napoleon's greatest and most lasting achievements were not made on the battlefield, but at home in his domestic policies. In 1800, Napoleon created the Bank of France, which helped the country to come out of the economic depression caused by the revolution. Before the Bank of France, financial power had been in the hands of about fifteen banking houses that had come from Switzerland in the mid-1700s. These bankers had been responsible for much of the agitation leading up to the revolution, and they also helped to orchestrate the rise of Napoleon, whom they hoped would restore stability and order. In return for their help, Napoleon gave them a monopoly over French finance through control of the Bank of France. The bank offered low interest loans and issued bank notes that helped to restart the economy.

In accordance with the spirit of the revolution, Napoleon oversaw the codification of a new system of laws that tore down the feudal system of noble privileges and established the equality of every man before the law. This system was called the Civil Code, and it remains the basis of French law and many other European legal systems to this day. Inspired by the tradition of civil codification in the ancient world, particularly in the Roman Empire, Napoleon's Civil Code (later known as the Napoleonic Code) had also been influenced by the Age of Enlightenment and the ideas that had inspired the French Revolution.

Before the Civil Code, French law had varied by class. The royals, nobles, clergy, and common people were all judged using different laws or customs that varied by class and region. The Civil Code was written in a language understandable to all men in France, and was applied equally to every class. The Code was also applied to the territories that had fallen under French rule during Napoleon's conquests, and in many French colonies around the world. In most of these places, including France, the Civil Code remains the basis of law to this day.

Also, during his rule as First Consul, Napoleon signed an agreement with the Pope called the Concordat which made Catholicism the dominant—but not exclusive—religion of France. Though Napoleon was by no means religious, France was a predominately Catholic nation. Devout Catholics had come into opposition with the revolutionaries after they had annexed and sold off church land and properties. Napoleon reestablished the church-state relationship, which benefited Pope Pius VII and Napoleon, who understood the power of religion as a political instrument. Napoleon said, "Skillful conquerors have not got entangled with priests. They can both contain them and use them."

Napoleon was baptized as a Catholic in Corsica, but he had little use for religion in his personal life. During his time in Egypt, he studied and gained respect for the Prophet Muhammad, though this was probably due to his ability as a military leader and political figure rather than a genuine interest in Islam itself. His interest in religion was opportunistic. He once said, "It is by making myself Catholic that I brought peace to

Brittany and Vendee. It is by making myself Italian that I won minds in Italy. It is by making myself a Moslem that I established myself in Egypt. If I governed a nation of Jews, I should reestablish the Temple of Solomon."

Bureaucratic Overhaul

One of the key tenets of the Civil Code was a merit-based system of promotion, particularly in government service. This had been a key issue in Napoleon's own life, as his rise through the military had been based upon his skills as a military strategist and a leader might not have been possible without the exodus of military officers that had accompanied the Revolution. Previously, bloodlines had largely determined the extent to which a man could rise within French society, but the Revolution had sought to put merit above blood. He said, "My motto has always been a career open to all talents without distinctions of birth."

Napoleon even created the Legion of Merit to reward men of great accomplishment and encourage achievement.

Napoleon believed in equality, but he did not favor those who demanded liberty. Opposition to his rule was crushed, and those who spoke against him were silenced. He believed that the common people had no use for liberty, or that if they had it they wouldn't know what to do with it. Under his rule, the parliament became irrelevant, and free elections were rigged in his favor. "I had been nourished by reflecting on liberty," Napoleon said, "But I thrust it aside when it obstructed my path."

At Home with Josephine

In 1803, France was still at peace and Napoleon had absolute power. With Napoleon serving as First Consul, Josephine took on the role of First Lady. She preferred to live in the country house at Malmaison because she feared the palaces in Paris were haunted with the ghosts of the dead monarchs executed during the Revolution. Napoleon joined her at Malmaison, making it his countryside seat of government. There he worked seven days a week, often eighteen hours a day. He was known for sleeping only a few hours a night, especially during military campaigns, but his high energy work ethic continued as he worked on his domestic policies and the creation of the Civil Code. Still, if he ever did relax it was at Malmaison with Josephine. She had warmed to him a great deal since the early days of their marriage, and he had given her security and a newfound status the likes of which she had never previously conceived.

England, Always England

The peace treaty between France and Great Britain was seen by all as weak and certain to be broken. On May 18, 1803, Great Britain declared war on France, to little surprise. France had established itself as the great land power in Europe, but England dominated the seas. After the French fleet's defeat at the Battle of the Nile, Napoleon tried to rebuild the French Navy in anticipation for his planned invasion of Great Britain, but the French navy was no match for the British. Indeed, an amphibious invasion of Great Britain by France, a plan that had been in the works for years, was eventually determined to be impossible.

The British Navy defended the coast of the English Channel, and the French Army ran drills and encamped on the French coast. The two powers were at a stalemate. Britain's sea power allowed it to take advantage of its colonial wealth, while the French relied upon their conquered territories on the European continent. England's Army was accustomed to fighting short tactical battles close to coastlines where they could retreat to their ships if necessary. They did not believe their military could defeat Napoleon on land.

Napoleon was feared in all of Europe. British cartoonists drew caricatures of Napoleon, depicting him as a short, fat Corsican rube, but British mothers told their children to pray that God protect them from the evil Napoleon, believing that an invasion was imminent. In late 1804 and early 1805, Britain began forming a new coalition. Sweden, Russia, and Austria (seeking revenge after their two defeats at the hands of Napoleon) signed an alliance with Great Britain. Napoleon had already begun concentrating a massive army in Boulogne on the English Channel in preparation for an invasion of Britain, but with the formation of the Third Coalition, the stage was set for another conflict between Napoleon and his European adversaries.

Chapter 4:

Expansion

"Power is my mistress. I have worked too hard at her conquest to allow anyone to take her away from me."

—**Napoleon Bonaparte**

To Empire

Following the assassination attempts perpetrated by the Bourbon Royalists and his subsequent consolidation of power, Napoleon began to imagine himself as an emperor in the likeness of Julius Caesar or Alexander the Great. He wanted to be on an equal standing with the great monarchs of Europe, but he did not have a crown. On a cold day in December of 1804, Napoleon brought the Pope to Paris to coronate him as the Emperor of France and Josephine as his queen. Napoleon meticulously orchestrated a proclamation by the senate, a vote of the people gave him political legitimacy, and the Pope gave him the religious legitimacy. At thirty-five, he became Emperor of France.

A half million French came out on that cold day in December to watch the empirical procession as it made its way through Paris. Napoleon wore a golden laurel wreath similar to the famous headdress worn by Caesar. When he and Josephine approached the Pope at the altar of Notre Dame, Napoleon himself took the empirical crown from the Pope, a replica of the crown of Charlemagne, and placed it on his own head.

Napoleon became the most powerful man at the head of the most powerful country in Europe. He again used the political power of religion to secure his legitimacy, not only in the eyes of Roman Catholic France, but also in the eyes of the monarchs of Europe who could no longer dispute his legitimacy on the grounds of religious ordination. He said, "As soon as a man becomes a king he is set apart from all other men. I always felt that Alexander the Great's idea of pretending to be descended from a god was inspired by a sure instinct for real politics."

Napoleon's Civic Code made law of the ideals of the Revolution, now the Pope's coronation confirmed that the changes of the revolution were ordained by God. "I am the instrument of providence," Napoleon said, "She will use me as long as I accomplish her designs. Then she will break me like a glass."

The Pinnacle of Power

Napoleon had reached the peak of his power. He began as an ambitious artillery lieutenant and rose to the rank of general through his aggressive leadership and ingenious strategy. He had married the woman he loved and made her his queen. His victories on the battlefield had given him the glory he needed to maintain his political power during his rise in France, and his skills as a propagandist and politician had placed him among the great houses of Europe. His ambition and his confidence in himself made him believe that he was invincible.

Napoleon was amassing an army on the English Channel in preparation for an invasion of England. He had 200,000 troops, but the 2,000 ships he needed to cross the channel were behind in construction as the British declared war and formed a coalition with the remaining European powers. Napoleon believed that if he could cross the Channel victory would be his. The British Army was no match in a ground campaign against the French. "If I'm master of the Channel for six hours," Napoleon said, "I'll be master of the world."

Napoleon was feared by the British, who believed he was truly capable of anything, but Napoleon needed ships to challenge the British dominance of the English Channel. By August of 1805, he realized his invasion of Britain would not be possible. He mustered his troops and paraded them along the coastline late in the summer of 1805, and then ordered them to turn away from England and march into the continent.

War of the Third Coalition

Austria and Russia had joined Britain in an alliance to destroy Napoleon and his empire. Tens of thousands of Russian soldiers marched across the continent to link up with the Austrians. Napoleon was in the midst of a war that had begun at the start of the French Revolution. The European monarchs all knew the fate of King Louis XVI, who'd been beheaded at the hands of the Paris mob. They feared the revolution would spread to their countries and that they might share the same fate. For the monarchs, the French Revolution was an existential crisis, a challenge to their power. Then Napoleon became the personification of the revolution in a single man. Napoleon brought with him to his conquered territories the ideals of the Revolution and his Civil Code, a direct challenge to the God-given authority of the monarchies.

The army Napoleon had formed at Boulogne became his Grand Army as it turned to face Europe. It totaled 350,000 men organized into seven corps of well-equipped and well trained soldiers eager to fight after months of preparations for an invasion of Britain. Each corps was fitted with 35 to 40 artillery pieces, and each was capable of independent action. They had been trained to fight from a strong defensive position for at least a day until another unit could come in to reinforce them.

Napoleon sent each corps out, separated by some distance. If one corps encountered an enemy it would take up a defensive position and hold until another, hearing the sound of gunfire, could come to its aid, usually from a flanking position that would immediately give the advantage to the French. Along with the infantry, Napoleon brought 22,000 cavalry as they set out to fight again in Europe. It was one of the largest armies ever seen.

In an attempt to clear the English Channel of the Royal Navy, Napoleon had sent the French Navy to attack the British in the Caribbean. He hoped this would divert the Royal Navy long enough for a joint French and Spanish naval attack on the remaining British fleet, allowing his ground troops access to the British Isles. This plan failed, however, when the French and Spanish naval coalition encountered the British fleet off the coast of Spain on their return from the Caribbean in the Battle of Cape Finisterre. The result of the battle was indecisive, but French Admiral Villeneuve failed to link up with the rest of the fleet for an attack on the British in the Channel.

After the naval failure in the Channel, Napoleon focused on the advancing armies on the continent. He planned to attack the Astro-Russian alliance before they could make an attempt to invade French territory. His men were superbly trained and feared in Europe. Many were veterans of the Italian campaign and the wars in the Rhineland, but others were young grunts who had been drafted into the army.

Napoleon's army was significant because it was the first time in history that an army in an ostensibly free society had been created with compulsory service rather than professional soldiers. Many of the young recruits were farmer's sons. They were attached to regiments of veteran troops who helped in their training.

A key element of Napoleon's tactics was the speed of his march. His soldiers would begin marching at dawn, and would not stop until the sun had disappeared. One soldier said, "The emperor has discovered a new way of making war. He uses our legs instead of our bayonets." By moving quickly, he could surprise the enemy, not only in their first encounter, but also when the reinforcement arrived hours later at the enemy flank. His men were capable of marching thirty miles a day, a speed that gave them a significant tactical advantage, particularly in Third Coalition campaign. This speed mimicked the similarly effective tactics of Julius Caesar, who was known for incredibly fast forced marches that had won him Gaul centuries before.

The Grand Army did not need a support element, another distinct advantage. It had no supply train leading back to France. The men foraged as they marched, adding to their speed and maneuverability.

Napoleon was indeed a short man, but he was only slightly shorter than the average height of men at the time. At 5'2", he often looked shorter in images where he was depicted standing among his elite Grenadiers (now called the Imperial Guard) who were required to be at least 6' tall. Despite his stature, he commanded great respect from his troops, who idolized him and yearned for his praise. To show approval, he would give a brave soldier a warmhearted tug on the ear. Napoleon once asked, "Who is the bravest man in this unit?" The men pointed to a soldier, and Napoleon took the Legion of

Honor off his own coat and pinned on him. As a keen motivator, the soldiers felt he was one of them. They trusted him and were willing to die for him, which made them quite a force to contend with on the battlefield.

Napoleon worked his men hard, and he continued to work hard himself. He was known to ride on horseback for ten hours, not once dismounting, even to eat. He slept very little, and at night he pored over maps of the battlefield and reports on enemy movements, studying each detail, including previous battles fought in the region and the tactics of the generals who fought there. When he was not writing orders, he found time to express his love for Josephine in letters. As the fall of 1805 came upon Europe, Napoleon moved further into the continent, preparing to face an allied army that outnumbered his two to one if he could not intercept the Austrians before they joined with the Russians.

The Austrians and the Russians believed they could defeat Napoleon through superior numbers, but Napoleon knew they were still spread out on the continent, and had not yet consolidated their forces. He knew that if he could strike the Austrians first, he could regain the advantage. On September 25, 1805, after a hasty and covert march, Napoleon crossed the Rhine with a front of 160 miles. Austrian commander Karl Mack had gathered the majority of his forces at a fortress called Ulm in Swabia (Southeastern Germany). Napoleon's wide front closed in around Mack, flanking him on all sides. Several minor engagements culminated in the Battle of Ulm, which ended with just 2,000 French casualties and the capture of 60,000 Austrian troops. "I did not intend to fight any but the English," Napoleon told Mack, "Until your master came along and provoked me. All empires come to an end." It was a great victory for Napoleon, but he soon received word of another French naval defeat at the hands of the Royal Navy at the Battle of Trafalgar. The French Navy, devastated after a series of terrible defeats by the Royal Navy, capitulated dominance of the sea to the British for the rest of the Napoleonic Wars.

Napoleon moved toward Vienna, and captured the city in November. Tsar Alexander I, in command of the Russian Army in Europe along with Francis II of the Holy Roman Empire decided to engage Napoleon in battle.

Napoleon slowed in Vienna, parading his troops through the streets and portraying himself as a representative of the French Revolution. He had taken his massive army over 500 miles in just 40 days, and had already defeated half the Austrian Army. But winter was fast approaching and the Russians still moved to join with the Austrians in a massive counter-offensive against the French. Napoleon was deep in hostile territory with an army that didn't have a supply train. Prussia was also beginning to signal it might enter the war. Finally, on November 22, the Russians linked up with the Austrians to form an army to take on Napoleon.

Austerlitz

Napoleon was faced with two choices: he could turn back or face the superior forces of the Austrian and Russian alliance. But Napoleon was not known for turning around, especially when a glorious battle could be had. As the winter began to set in, Napoleon began to survey the battlefield. He especially studied the battles of Fredrick the Great, who had waged war in the region in the mid-1700s. Finally, he selected a hilly field surrounded by woods and ponds, a place not far from the small village of Austerlitz. It was here that

Napoleon would make his stand against the Allies. He told his generals, "Gentlemen, examine this ground carefully. It is going to be a battleground. You will have a part to play upon it."

70,000 Russians joined by 20,000 Austrians faced Napoleon's 75,000 troops. The remainder of the Grand Army was stationed across the territories already won. The Russians were commanded by Tsar Alexander I, who at just 28 was eager to see his first victory in battle, particularly if that victory came over Napoleon. However, he was inexperienced and arrogant, faults that did not go unexploited by one of the greatest military strategists of all time.

Napoleon planned to lure the Tsar into attacking him. Before the battle, Napoleon had secured the high ground, known as the Pratzen heights. But, on December 2—the one year anniversary of his coronation as emperor—Napoleon ceded the high ground, redeploying his troops below the Pratzen heights, hoping the Tsar would take the bait.

Napoleon was taking a serious risk by giving up the high ground to the enemy. In Napoleon's day, warfare demanded a strategic positioning of forces, and the high ground usually gave a significant advantage to the army that could secure it. Napoleon was making a calculated risk, however. He said to his staff, "If I wanted to stop the enemy, it is there [the Pratzen Heights] that I should position myself. But that would lead to only an ordinary battle, and I want decisive success."

The Russians took up position on the Pratzen, and the Tsar called a Council of War with his General to discuss their plan of attack. Alexander interpreted Napoleon's retreat from the heights as a sign of weakness, and lobbied for an immediate attack, but one of his more experienced generals—the hard drinking, one-eyed General Kutuzov—objected to the plan, suspecting that Napoleon was laying a trap. The Tsar disregarded Kutuzov's warning, however, and ordered the attack. Napoleon's bait was taken.

The night before the attack, Napoleon was in high spirits. He dined on potatoes fried with onions, his favorite meal, and inspected the troops. He told an aide, "This is the finest evening of my life." In the morning, a dense fog had overtaken the battlefield, shielding the French troops stationed in the low lands. The Russian position on the heights was visible as the Pratzen lifted above the fog. Napoleon's soldiers were still tired from the incredible march they'd undertaken in the six weeks prior, but they were eager to do battle on behalf of their emperor.

Poor organization by the advancing Russian columns slowed the attack on the French below. The Tsar had ordered the allies off the high ground toward the far end of Napoleon's weaker right flank, located at a village called Tellnitz. Napoleon had anticipated this move, and had rushed two divisions under the command of Davout from Vienna in the days leading up to the battle. Davout brought 12,000 men 70 miles in just two days. In Tellnitz, Davout met with a superior Russian force, but he was able to defend the town long enough to protect Napoleon's right flank, thereby giving Napoleon time to attack the now undefended Pratzen. As the sun rose, Napoleon's 17,000 troops began marching up to take the hill. "So far the enemy is behaving like they are conducting maneuvers on my orders," Napoleon said during the battle.

On the top of the hill, Tsar Alexander told his staff, "They come out of a clear sky," to which an aide replied, "Your majesty, you should rather say: 'They come from hell.'" From that moment on, the battle fell into Napoleon's hands. His strategy had worked, and the Tsar panicked at the quick shift in advantage, fled his command, leaving the Russian Army in a chaotic retreat as Napoleon's troops began firing down on the exposed Russians from both their flanks. Napoleon had predicted just such an outcome: "One sharp blow, and the war is over," he'd said. By 9:30 that morning, the French controlled the Pratzen heights and swept across the battlefield, attacking the enemy from behind.

By 5:00 that evening, the battle was over. The French had suffered 9,000 killed or wounded, and the Russians and Austrians had a combined 16,000 casualties. The Tsar and his army retreated in defeat, but Francis II, the Austrian Emperor, came himself to sue for peace with Napoleon.

There was great rejoicing in Paris when they learned of Napoleon's victory. He wrote Josephine, "I have beaten the Austro-Russian army commanded by the two emperors. I am a little weary."

France and Austria signed the Treaty of Pressburg on December 4, in which Austria agreed to recognize the territories captured by Napoleon in his previous campaign against the Austrians. After the battle, Napoleon told his troops, "Soldiers I am pleased with you. You have decorated your eagles with immortal glory. You will be greeted with joy, and it will be enough for you to say, 'I was at the battle of Austerlitz,' for people to reply, 'There goes a brave man.'"

Victory, but the War Continues

After the defeat of the Austrians and Russians, peace seemed at hand, but six months after Austerlitz, Napoleon was still in the heart of Europe preparing for war. In 1806, he established the Confederation of the Rhine, which was to act as a buffer between Prussia and France, and effectively brought an end to the Holy Roman Empire. With France's new holdings moving closer to Prussia, the Prussians declared war on France.

Napoleon expressed his feelings on the growing French Empire, saying, "Among the established sovereigns, war aims never to go beyond possession of a province or a fortress. With me, the stake is always my existence and that of the whole empire. Conquest alone made me what I am. Conquest alone can keep me there." Some historians believe that Napoleon's victory at Austerlitz inflated his ego to the point that he began to lose touch with reality. He had already defeated the strongest militaries in Europe, but nothing seemed to quench his thirst for conquest, even if it meant sacrificing countless French citizens in the process and risking the stability of the nation. On the other hand, some suggest that Napoleon's desire for conquest and glory aligned with the desires of the French people, and their willingness to follow Napoleon into battle was based on their desire to reach the same level of power and glory, if only vicariously through the life of their emperor.

The Prussian desire to meet Napoleon in battle was quickly put down. Napoleon invaded Prussia with 180,000 troops. Following his well-established strategy, Napoleon quickly marched into the country in an effort to isolate and destroy Prussian resistance before they had time to consolidate their forces. The French won decisive victories at the Battles of Jena and Auerstedt on October 14, 1806. Before the engagement, Napoleon had said, "The idea that the Prussians could take the field alone against me seems so ridiculous that it does not merit discussion." In under three weeks, Napoleon crushed the Prussian Army, taking 140,000 prisoners and inflicting 25,000 casualties. Napoleon then marched through Berlin, again espousing the ideals of the French Revolution as he went.

Down with the Monarchy, Up with the Bonapartes

He had now spread his ideology far into Europe. Only Great Britain and Russia stood in his way, but in the rest of Europe his Civil Code and the abolition of feudal privileges began to spread and take hold with each conquered nation he paraded through. Still, he did not favor liberty. "I have come to realize that men are not born to be free," he said. "Liberty is a need felt by a small class of people whom nature has endowed with nobler minds than the mass of men." Napoleon did not advocate liberty for every man, but he certainly thought himself deserving. He believed in his own character, the destiny he saw for himself, and how that destiny, whether by fate or by luck, aligned with the destiny of France. He lived in forty-four palaces across Europe and lived like the king he wanted to be. He made his brothers and sisters the new royalty. His brother Louis became the King of Holland. Joseph became the King of Naples, and Jerome the King of Westphalia. His sister Caroline became a queen, Pauline a princess, and Alicia a duchess. His mother was given the title Madame Mar. "I need my family to stabilize my dynasty," Napoleon said, "If I distributed thrones according to merit I should have made different choices."

Napoleon stayed close to his mother her entire life, and had immense respect for her. She was impressed with his incredible success, but she was worried it would not last. Josephine was still uncomfortable living in the conquered palaces of the former royal families, and continued to spend her time at Malmaison. There she tended her gardens, importing exotic plants, trees, and flowers from across the world. Despite Napoleon's continued affairs, he remained attached to her. She told a friend, "He considers me one of the rays of his star." Josephine made an admirable empress. Napoleon said, "I win the wars, and she wins people's hearts." Josephine, whether by necessity or simply the passage of time, had fallen more in love with Napoleon than she'd ever been before. She became jealous of his mistresses, and he became irritated with her immense spending (one million francs a year on clothes alone).

Napoleon said of his other women, "My mistresses do not engage my feelings. Power is my mistress." When Josephine became upset with Napoleon's indiscretion, he could not understand why she was upset. "She takes things far too seriously," He said, "She is afraid that I shall fall deeply in love. Can she not understand that love is not for me?" If Napoleon did love anyone, it was most certainly Josephine. Together they'd risen to power and created a partnership. Josephine's only fault was out of her control: she hadn't given Napoleon a son.

War of the Fourth Coalition

After their defeat, the Prussians had refused to negotiate with the French, hoping the Russians would again enter the war and change the momentum. After his victory over the Prussians in November 1806, Napoleon imposed the first elements of his Continental System through the Berlin Decree. The Continental System was an attempt to prohibit trade between continental Europe and Great Britain. Napoleon hoped to use economic sanctions to weaken British power, but they were difficult to enforce and violated often.

Napoleon marched into Poland in the winter of 1806-1807 to meet the advancing Russian army. In February, he met the Russians at the Battle of Eylau, which resulted in a stalemate and a great number of losses on both sides. For a time, the two sides separated to consolidate and replenish their forces. Then, in June of 1807 the Russians and French met again at the battle of Friedland.

Napoleon had marched deep into Poland, just 100 miles from the Russian border. The bloody battle at Eylau had been Napoleon's response to a surprise attack by the Russians when Napoleon was still in Warsaw. The Tsar Alexander wanted revenge against Napoleon after his defeat at the Battle of Austerlitz, and Napoleon wanted to crush the Russian Tsar once and for all after the remainder of his army had escaped during their previous engagement. They met again at the Battle of Friedland. It was an extremely bloody battle where the already weakened Russians met Napoleon's strengthened army. Seventy-thousand killed or wounded were reported from both sides, but the Russian Army had been completely devastated. "It is not combat anymore," a Russian general wrote the Tsar, "it is butchery." Napoleon's army was badly injured, but Alexander's was nearly gone.

With almost no army left to defend against an invasion and the French just miles from the Russian border, Alexander considered what to do next. Alexander's brother, Duke Constantine encouraged the Tsar to make peace, saying, "Sire, if you are considering fighting the French, you might as well consider giving each soldier a gun and letting him put a bullet in his head. The result will be the same."

On June 25, 1807, Alexander went to Tilsit, a town on Russia's western border. To signify their equal status and the new border between the French and Russian Empires, the two leaders met on a raft anchored at the center of the River Neiman, which was the natural western border of the Russian Empire. The Tsar wanted to find a peaceful solution that would also benefit him. The first thing he said to Napoleon was, "Sir, I hate the English as much as you do," to which Napoleon said, "Then we have just made peace."

Napoleon gave the Russians fairly generous peace terms, especially compared to the Prussians, who had finally come to negotiate with Napoleon. The Prussians saw more than half their territories taken from them as Napoleon created new kingdoms and countries and handed their thrones to his siblings. Russia, however, only lost a few island territories and was forced to withdraw troops from Wallachia and Moldavia. Importantly, Napoleon demanded that the Russians join the Continental System and become France's ally in a gambit to economically pressure the British into a peace agreement.

During the peace talks, Napoleon and Alexander I spent a great deal of time together. After several days, they seemed to become friends, inspecting each other armies, awarding medals to soldiers on both sides, and discussing their leadership ideas. Napoleon seemed infatuated with Alexander, describing him as handsome, like a hero with all the grace of an amiable Parisian. The Tsar seemed in awe of Napoleon's power and interested to learn about his techniques. After their extended peace talks, Napoleon was certain he'd made a friend of Alexander. He wrote Josephine, "If Alexander were a woman, I would make him my mistress."

However, Napoleon's belief in the friendship with Alexander proved to be a huge mistake. Alexander had never intended to keep his word in their agreement, and his amiable demeanor at Tilsit had likely been a clever ruse to seduce Napoleon into more favorable terms. Napoleon thought he had charmed Alexander, but in fact it was the other way around.

Summit of Greatness

In 1807, Paris again celebrated. They were overjoyed at the treaty between France and Russia. Peace in Europe was once again achieved, and France's power was at an all-time high. Napoleon ruled over 70,000,000 French, Italian, Dutch, German, and Polish people. His new empire was the greatest since Rome. His victories over Russia and Prussia were so great that Napoleon began to believe he was incapable of making a mistake or being wrong. Napoleon no longer (if he ever did) viewed himself in a realistic manner. He saw himself as a superman, someone protected by God, or someone divine. "Ambition is never content," Napoleon wrote, "Even on the summit of greatness."

Despite his near absolute power in Europe, Napoleon still felt he needed more conquest. Perhaps he still believed that his military victories were the key to his glory and his popular support, or perhaps he became addicted to the power he gained from defeating another army in battle. In either case, his desire for more power proved to be a devastating trait.

Chapter 5:
Overreaching

> *"Never interrupt your enemy when he is making a mistake."*
> —Napoleon Bonaparte

The Peninsular War

Napoleon began to focus his efforts on the implementation of the Continental System. The Portuguese under John VI had gone back on their policy with British trade. They had at first agreed to suspend trade with the British in their ports, but after the Franco-Spanish naval defeat at the Battle of Trafalgar, Portugal had again opened up trade with Great Britain. On October 17, 1807, Napoleon sent 24,000 French troops under the command of General Junot across the Pyrenees into Portugal to enforce Napoleon's Continental System. The French initially had the support of the Spanish monarch, but French agents began to interfere with the Spanish royal family in an attempt to destabilize the government. The French supported factions who attempted to rival the Spanish King for power. On March 24, 1807, Napoleon sent Marshal Murat into Spain with 120,000 troops to support one of these factions in an attempt to overthrow the Spanish crown. Within weeks, riots broke out in Madrid against the French occupation. Napoleon made his brother Joseph the King of Spain in the summer of 1808 against intense public opposition.

Napoleon believed that the spirit of the revolution that had allowed him to gain support in Italy and other conquered nations during his earlier conquests would have the same effect on the Spanish population, but Spain was not prepared for the concepts of equality and liberty that had spread across the rest of Europe in the previous years. The Spanish were still very conservative and staunchly Catholic. Napoleon had said, "With my banner bearing the words liberty and emancipation from superstition, I shall be regarded as the liberator of Spain." Instead, his troops were regarded as aggressors, and rather than rising up in a revolution against the monarchy, the Spanish people began to rise up against the French. On May 2, 1808, the Spanish people rose up against French troops in Madrid. By nightfall, 150 French soldiers were dead. The rebellion against the French occupation spread across the country in a prolonged war that lasted for the next six years.

The Spanish engaged in guerilla warfare. Small bands of Spanish patriots fought asymmetrically, in short, strategic engagements that disrupted French supply lines, decreased troop morale, and confined the French to the defense of fortifications and camps rather than large, decisive engagements with the enemy. The French had never fought this type of war, and they were not prepared for it. The conflict became long and brutal, and both sides committed atrocities against each other. The French tortured and maimed their Spanish prisoners, and the Spanish did the same to the French. A Spanish victory over the French at the Battle of Bailen broke the myth of Napoleonic invincibility, and gave the Spanish the motivation to continue to fight the French throughout their occupation.

Napoleon responded to this defeat by heading to Iberia himself in November of 1808, after the Congress of Erfurt where he had attempted to secure Russian allegiance in a future war with Austria. The Russians agreed to support Napoleon, and he quickly organized his Grand Army and crossed into Spain. In December, Napoleon led 80,000 troops into Madrid and met British troops, who had attempted to support the Spanish, in a battle that eventually drove them to the coast and caused them to exit the conflict. After his victory over the British in Spain, Napoleon left Iberia to deal with the Austrians. He never returned to Spain, but his armies there continued to fight Spanish resistance until 1814, when Allied forces in Spain, with the support of British troops led by the Duke of Wellington finally pushed the French out of the country.

A Son

Napoleon's actions in Spain revealed how power had come to blind his judgment. He began to refuse advice, and assumed the role of a god emperor, similar to Louis XVI, the last of the French Divine Right Monarchs. He realized he needed a successor to pass this authority on after his death. He needed a son, but Josephine was too old to give him one at forty-six. She knew her time as queen was coming to an end. She said, "I know I will be shamefully dismissed from the bed of the man who crowned me."

Napoleon still loved Josephine, and he did not want to give her up. His desire for a son who would one day carry on his legacy and maintain his empire became a greater urge. He told Josephine it was necessary to sacrifice their marriage for the greater glory of France. He divorced her, and after visiting her one last time at Malmaison, never saw her again. She received the country estate at Malmaison, and an allowance of three million francs a year.

Napoleon turned his attention toward finding a wife who could birth him a son. He said, "I want to marry a womb." He found the Archduchess Marie Louise, the 19 year old daughter of his arch enemy Emperor Francis I of Austria. Napoleon hoped to marry Louise for a son, but also to secure a position within the Hapsburg ruling family, one of the oldest and most powerful in Europe. Marie Louise hated Napoleon at first. She wrote in her diary, "Just to see the man would be the worst form of torture." Her father did not care about her objection, and forced Marie Louise to marry the Emperor and bring peace between France and Austria. On April 2, 1810, Emperor Napoleon Bonaparte married the Archduchess Marie Louise in an extravagant ceremony at Notre Dame.

Marie quickly warmed to the Emperor, writing her father, "He loves me very much, and I respond to his love sincerely. There is something very fetching and very eager about him that is impossible to resist." Napoleon successfully allied himself with the Hapsburg monarch through his marriage of Marie Louis. In a year, she gave him a son, whom Napoleon called "The King of Rome." At 42, he became a family man. He said, "Late hours, hardship, war, are not for me at my age. I love my bed, my repose, more than anything, but I must finish my work." It was becoming more difficult for Napoleon to maintain the level of energy and aggression that had propelled him to power through his earlier conquests. In 1811, his army was mired in Spain, and Britain remained at large. A new war was imminent, and Napoleon needed to rise again to the challenge.

Chapter 6:
Defeat and Collapse

"It requires more courage to suffer than to die."
—**Napoleon Bonaparte**

The War of the Fifth Coalition

In the years leading up to his marriage with Marie Louis, the Austrians attempted to avenge their defeat against the French. The Austrians hastily invaded Bavaria in French-controlled territory against the warnings of Archduke Charles and others who believed that Austria was not prepared to take on the empire. Napoleon was surprised by the Austrians' quick advance. The Grand Army was separated by 75 miles, and the Austrians advanced through the center. The Austrians attacked Marshal Davout at the Battle of Eckmuhl, which resulted in a victory for the French. On May 13, 1809, Vienna fell again to the French.

Though the Austrians lost Vienna, they had not lost many troops in the initial conflict, and they continued to fight. Archduke Charles met Napoleon at the Battle of Aspern-Essling, where the Austrians had 110,000 troops to Napoleon's 31,000. Between both sides there were 23,000 casualties, and Napoleon was eventually forced to retreat. The European allies were encouraged by this victory, because it was the first time Napoleon had been defeated in a pitched, open battle. After the defeat, Napoleon consolidated his forces and planned a massive attack. He led 180,000 troops across the Danube to meet Charles and the Austrians, who had assembled a force of 150,000 men.

The ensuing Battle of Wagram was the largest battle in Europe until that time. It lasted two days, with the French and Austrians both assaulting the other's flanks. The Austrian attack was less successful, and the steady assault by Napoleon's flanking attack eventually gave him an opportunity to attack the Austrian center, breaking their lines and causing Charles to order a chaotic retreat.

The British attempted to create a two-front war by landing troops in Holland to attack Napoleon there, while the majority of his forces were concentrated against the Austrians. However, the British troops landed in Holland after the French had already defeated the Austrians, and eventually succumbed to disease, which killed more than 4,000 British troops. The British effort merely postponed the Austrian peace talks with the French as they waited to see the outcome of the British intervention. The Austrians signed the Treaty of Schonbrunn in October of 1809, which allowed the Austrians to keep hereditary lands, but took many other regions of the Austrian Empire and distributed them among other French territories. The Austrians had lost nearly 3 million subjects in the Treaty, but they maintained the Hapsburg Empire. With the marriage of Marie Louise to Napoleon, they came to peace with France and entered into an alliance with him.

Invasion of Russia

After Tsar Alexander's treaty with Napoleon at Tilsit and the renewed alliance between France and Russia at the Congress of Erfut, the situation with Russia seemed stable. However, the Russian economy had been harmed by its agreement not to trade with Great Britain, and Russian nobles pressured the Tsar to break his agreement with Napoleon. Napoleon threatened serious consequences if the Russians join in an alliance with Britain, but Alexander went ahead with plans to invade Poland in 1812.

Napoleon received intelligence about the Tsar's preparations for war, and he began amassing what would be the largest army ever created. On June 23, 1812, against the advice of his generals, Napoleon led a combined army of Italians, Poles, Germans, and French totaling more than 450,000 men into Russia. Napoleon hoped to meet the bulk of the Russian Army in a single decisive battle, but the Russians only met Napoleon in a series of smaller engagements, where they quickly retreated and led him deeper into Russian territory.

The Russians avoided battle after battle and practiced a scorched earth tactic that destroyed towns and farmland in their wake and left nothing for the French Army to forage. The French Army was used to foraging and looting conquered lands to supply themselves, but the Russians took this ability away from them during their retreat into the heart of Russia. Finally, the Russians met Napoleon on September 7, 1812, at the Battle of Borodino, just outside of Moscow. It became the bloodiest battle in Europe up to that point, with 44,000 Russians and 35,000 French dead. Napoleon wrote of the battle, "The most terrible of all my battles was the one before Moscow. The French showed themselves to be worthy of victory, but the Russians showed themselves worthy of being invincible."

Napoleon believed taking Moscow would cause Alexander to admit defeat and sue for peace, but the Russians retreated through Moscow, and the governor, Feodor Rostopchin, ordered the city burned as the French began their occupation. Napoleon called upon Alexander to sign a peace treaty, but the Tsar did not respond to his request. Napoleon, realizing that he could no longer sustain his army in Russia, and hearing of an attempted coup in Paris, ordered his army to return to France.

They moved slowly back across the Russian plains and faced a treacherous march as the Russian Winter arrived early in November. He had already lost a great many troop to plague, desertion, and in battle against the Russians, and in their retreat he lost thousands more. Ten thousand were lost on one of the coldest days, when temperatures plummeted to 22 degrees below zero. Soldiers and horses froze in the icy snow, and the columns of troops were savagely attacked by Cossack militia and Russian serfs as they trudged along. "Our lips stuck together," one soldier wrote, "Our nostrils froze. We seemed to be marching in a world of ice." Soon their food ran out, and soldiers began to fight over dead horse meat. The army slowly fell apart, and Napoleon eventually deserted his army in order to return to Paris more quickly and defend his political position against a potential coup.

His army had begun at a strength of 400,000 soldiers. When it crossed the Berezina River out of Russia, it numbered only 40,000. It was a huge loss for Napoleon, and came to mark the beginning of his end.

War of the Sixth Coalition

With the French Army in ruins, the coalition powers were heartened, and Prussia, Austria, Sweden, Russia, Spain, Portugal, and Great Britain formed a new alliance to attack Napoleon on all sides. Napoleon believed a single great victory could change his luck and turn the odds in his favor. When he returned to France, he immediately raised an army of 350,000. He was fighting a war coming at him from every angle. He took command of the army in Germany and won a series of victories over the coalition, but as the allies began to mount troops on all sides of France, Napoleon quickly became hopelessly outnumbered. In the fall of 1813, the coalition met Napoleon at the Battle of Leipzig.

After the Russian disaster, the French army consisted of inexperienced troops, many of whom were teenagers. He fielded 160,000 men at Leipzig against the coalition's forces, which numbered 380,000 troops. Napoleon attempted to make an aggressive stance against the coalition in Leipzig, but his army was encircled by the allies. Pinned down and anticipating the loss of his entire army, Napoleon ordered a retreat out of Germany. His troops had to fight their way out of their poor position the whole way. Many of the Saxon troops who had fought under Napoleon as a part of the Confederation of the Rhine deserted to join the coalition, and thousands of French troops died when a bridge was prematurely destroyed as the French were still in retreat. The Battle of Leipzig was the largest military engagement until World War I. Between 90,000 and 110,000 troops were killed or missing. Napoleon retreated back to France with just 70,000 troops to defend against the coalition armies, which still advanced. Napoleon said, "A year ago the whole of Europe was marching alongside of us, today the whole of Europe is marching against us."

Napoleon continued to fight on in an effort to defend France, but in two months he'd lost 400,000 men. In November of 1813, Napoleon was offered peace that would allow him to remain Emperor and for France to retain control of Belgium, Savoy, and the Rhineland, but capitulate the rest of it territories. The allies explained these were the best terms that would be offered, and continued to surround France on all sides.

Napoleon, deluded into believing in his invincibility despite his horrendous position, still expected to win the war, and did not take the offered peace. In December, the allies withdrew their offer, and as 1814 began, Napoleon began to realize the gravity of his situation, and tried to reopen the peace offer. The British did not want Napoleon to remain in power, and they pushed into France from the south. Napoleon won several small victories as the coalition surrounded Paris, but they simply did not have enough men to change the tide of the war. Outnumbered three to one, the leaders of Paris surrendered in March of 1814.

Before the surrender, Napoleon began to burn his private papers. Even Marie Louise's father, Francis I, had turned against Napoleon, and the coalition forces had invaded France itself. "Don't worry," Napoleon tried to reassure his wife and son, "We shall beat papa Francis.

Trust me." But on March 31, 1814, the Russians and coalition army marched through the streets of Paris. The Senate in Paris believed the coalition was fighting not against France, but against Napoleon, and on April 1 they voted to dethrone the Emperor in an act called the Emperor's Demise. On April 4, Napoleon attempted to hand the throne to his son with Marie Louise as the regent, but the Coalition denied this attempt. The same day, General Ney, learning of the Senate's action, had refused to follow Napoleon in an effort to retake Paris. The soldiers wanted to fight on for their emperor, but the officers knew victory was impossible. On April 12, 1814, Napoleon unconditionally abdicated his throne. His secretary wrote, "His majesty appeared to be entirely crushed. His agitation was often so great that, without being aware of it, he tore at his leg with his nails until the blood flowed."

During his retreat through Russia, Napoleon began to carry a small leather pouch containing poison he intended to use if he was captured. On the evening of his abdication, he poured the poison into a glass of wine and drank it, but the poison failed to kill him.

Exile to Elba

Napoleon lived to see the breakup of his empire. Marie Louise and his son were taken to Austria. He never saw them again. The persistence of the rest of Europe to stop the spread of the French Empire finally succeeded. Napoleon's own aggression, along with his belief in himself as invincible and his divine destiny to bring Europe into a new age caused him to act recklessly, and this eventually led to disaster. As he left his palace at Fontainebleau on April 20 to enter his exile, he addressed his Imperial Guard one last time. "Goodbye my children," Napoleon said, "I am leaving. Do not grieve over my fate. I would like to press all of you close to my heart. Let me at least embrace your banner." He took the flag of the Guard in his hand and kissed it. "Let this kiss resonate in the hearts of all my soldiers. Farewell once again. Let this last kiss enter into all your hearts."

A British warship carried Napoleon into exile on the Island of Elba, a few miles off the Tuscan coast. On his way to Elba, the ship passed Corsica, a reminder of how far Napoleon had come. At 45, he had risen to control the largest Empire in Europe since the time of Rome, and he had lived to see it all collapse. He was allowed to retain his title as Emperor, and became Napoleon, Emperor of the Isle Elba. He was given a villa on the sea, and spent his time on Elba creating an iron works, developing the military and agriculture on the island. At first he had been depressed when he arrived on Elba, but he soon regained his urge to take action. He planted olive and mulberry trees, organized a garbage collection service, and made new laws, such as a requirement for the peasants on the island to sleep no more than five to a bed. While on Elba, Napoleon learned that Josephine had died at Malmaison. He did not leave his room for two days.

In France, the coalition restored the Bourbon monarchy. King Louis XVIII came to power under a constitutional monarchy, but the king was weak, and did not have the traits that had secured popular support for Napoleon. The royalist threatened to take away the revolution's gains, and the economy began to lurch. The king was unpopular, and Napoleon waited for ten months on Elba for an opportunity to make a move. He received word that the British were intending to send him to another, more remote island in the Atlantic Ocean, and so, on February 28, 1815,

Napoleon escaped Elba on a brig called the Inconstant. He evaded capture by French and British ships, and returned to France two days later with 700 men. "After making a mistake, or suffering a misfortune," Napoleon said, "The man of genius always gets back on his feet."

Chapter 7:

Last Stand

"If you want a thing done well, do it yourself."
—**Napoleon Bonaparte**

100 Days

The king, upon hearing of Napoleon's escape and entrance into France, sent the 5th Regiment under General Ney to meet Napoleon and bring him into custody. When Ney's troops approached Napoleon on March 7, 1815, the former emperor dismounted his horse and approached the soldiers alone. When he came close, he said, "Here I am. Kill your Emperor if you wish." The soldier responded with, "Long live the Emperor," and Ney himself, who had promised the King he would bring Napoleon to Paris in an iron cage, kissed Napoleon and fell in behind him as they turned to march on Paris.

When King Louis XVIII learned of Ney's betrayal, he fled to Belgium, aware of his unpopularity and weak political support. Two weeks later, with growing military support, Napoleon arrived in Paris, and established his new government in a period known as the 100 Days. The rest of Europe was shocked by Napoleon's quick return to power. By June, Napoleon had amassed 200,000 troops to support his new government. His enemies rightly panicked.

The Coalition met in Vienna to come to an agreement on the shape of post-Napoleonic Europe. The meeting had been marked by conflict and disagreement, but, upon learning of Napoleon's return, they immediately united to assemble an army that could quickly crush Napoleon and stop another French advance through Europe. Great Britain, Prussia, Austria, and Russia again united to take on Napoleon.

The odds were against Napoleon from the beginning. All of Europe had lined up against him. They saw him as a disturber of peace, and they wanted to stop him quickly. France did not stand a chance against the entire coalition, but Napoleon believed he could win if he could reach the British Army in Belgium and destroy it before it was reinforced by the Prussians, the tactic that had worked for him so many times before. The Austrians and Russians were also on the move across Europe, but Napoleon would try, as he had in the past, to win by isolating and destroying his enemies individually. It was a daring plan, and likely to fail, but in June Napoleon moved his Army of the North into Belgium to attack.

The Battle of Waterloo

Napoleon planned to gamble his survival on one decisive victory, much as he had in the past. He needed to wedge his army between the British and their Prussian reinforcements before they could link up with the Russians and Austrians. Each Coalition army had pledged 150,000 troops in the effort to defeat Napoleon, and Napoleon's 200,000 men stood no chance against a combined assault. The British in Belgium were led by the Duke of Wellington, an aristocratic general who was arrogant, but unflinching. The British were known for their strong naval power, but their infantry was known to fight short battles near the coast, where they could quickly retreat to their ships if they began to lose.

Napoleon hoped to exploit this tendency in Wellington, and chose a place called Waterloo for the battle that would decide his fate. It was an open field about three mile wide and one mile long. Wellington had 68,000 men, and needed the assistance of Marshall Blucher's 72,000 Prussians if he was to win the day against Napoleon. With Blucher, the Coalition forces outnumbered Napoleon's two to one, but Blucher was still miles away from the impending battle as the British and French forces coalesced at Waterloo. Wellington sent a message to Blucher, "My God, come as fast as you can. We'll fight to the last moment and the last man."

The night before the battle, the soldiers had to sleep under pouring rain. In the morning, everyone was soaking wet, and the battlefield was muddy and dotted with puddles. Napoleon waited until around 11:00AM to begin his attack, possibly because his wanted to allow time for the battlefield to dry out, or because he was suffering from some sort of ailment. As the hours passed, Blucher got closer to Waterloo, and the French position became direr. Napoleon had sent a large force to find and assault Blucher before he reached the battle, but it was unclear whether or not this was effective until much later in the day.

Before the battle began, as Napoleon stared out over the wet field before him, he later recalled, "I felt that fortune was abandoning me. I no longer had the feeling that I was sure to succeed."

Finally, at 11:30 AM, Napoleon's artillery opened fire. Napoleon planned to assault Wellington's positions at two farm houses on both sides of the battlefield and the crest of a ridge at the center. Napoleon believed that Wellington's center was located at one of these farm houses, a place called Hougoumont. French and British troops fought all afternoon for control of the farmhouse. Napoleon hoped to draw Wellington's reserve troops in to support the center position at Hougoumont, but eventually Napoleon had to send his own reserves there to support his attack on it. Even worse, Napoleon had miscalculated Wellington's center. It was actually located to the east of Hougoumont, cleverly hidden behind the crest of a ridge. The British repelled successive attacks at Hougoumont for several hours. Meanwhile, Napoleon ordered his infantry to attack what he believed to be the British right flank. Through this action, Napoleon hoped to drive himself between Wellington and Blucher, who was approaching from the east.

Wellington's infantry fought against the French as they approached the ridge. Both sides sustained heavy losses, but it appeared as if the British lines might crumble over the superior numbers of the French. Seeing the imperiled infantry, the British cavalry under General Uxbridge organized unseen behind the crest of the hill, and charged the French infantry to repel their attack. Chaos ensued as the British cavalry moved across the entire battlefield, attacking advancing French battalions as they went. They sustained heavy casualties, but remained active in the battle for the rest of the day.

After the British counterattack against the French infantry, General Ney believed the British position on the top of the hill was weakened, because he mistakenly took retreating wounded infantry for a general retreat. He ordered his cavalry to attack the hill, though he had little infantry support available. He believed he could break Wellington's center with the French cavalry alone, but Wellington still had reserves hidden behind the crest of the hill, and he ordered them to form into a defensive square—a deadly defense against unsupported cavalry. Ney ordered assault after assault on the British infantry behind the hill, but the squares held firm, and repelled the French attacks. The French cavalry sustained heavy losses in the repeated attacks, and their failure to destroy the British cannon they had overtaken on the hill meant that when their retreat began, they were bombarded further by cannon fire.

On the other side of the field from Hougomount was La Haye Sainte, another farm complex that was defended by German elements under British command. All morning, the British had defended the position against sustained assault by the French, but as Ney began his assault on Wellington's center, D'Erlon led a French assault on La Haye Saint that proved successful, largely because the Germans ran out of ammunition. With La Haye Saint under French control, the French were within 60 yards of the British center, and some skirmishers were close enough to begin firing on Wellington's command post. Wellington lost most of his general staff during the engagement, and had to relocate his command after La Haye Saint fell.

Despite the success of the infantry squares deployed by the British against the French cavalry, Ney's sustained attack and the capture of La Haye Saint now put those same infantry within range of musket and artillery fire. The British sustained heavy losses from some of the squares that came into range of French artillery that had moved up on the battlefield. Napoleon now had a chance to break the allied center, but some Prussian elements had already begun to arrive on the battlefield.

Napoleon's motto had always been, "Never attack a man in a prepared position." Napoleon's latter battles were marked by a lack of imagination that many of his earlier successes had been based upon. He had attacked the British center in a frontal assault, and now the French cavalry was almost completely destroyed. Just as Napoleon saw an opportunity to crush the remaining British forces, who were now extremely weak and on the verge of collapse, the Prussians began to appear on the horizon.

Napoleon ordered his feared Imperial Guard to attack the British center, hoping to quickly destroy Wellington's remaining forces so he could turn and fight the Prussians. Line after line of Guardsmen advanced on the British center. Wellington had already called up the remainder of his reserves, and Napoleon did the same. In a single minute, the first charge of the guard saw 400 of them fall, but they kept advancing. They nearly broke through the British line, but Wellington's men stood fast.

It was too late. The Prussians rushed to Wellington's aid and began attacking Napoleon's right flank. The Guard was defeated for the first time in the Napoleonic Wars, and word quickly spread through the other ranks that they were in retreat. Morale was crushed, and the French army, sustaining

41,000 killed, wounded, or missing, had lost, and was in full retreat.

Blucher reached the battle just in time to save Wellington. He had won the battle for the Allies. Napoleon tried in vain to rally his retreating troops to make one last stand, but he soon realized that all was lost, and he fled the battlefield to evade capture. He returned to Paris, where he found that the legislature and the people had turned against him. On June 22, just days after Waterloo, he abdicated his throne for a second time. He went to Malmaison, where he settled for several days. The Coalition forces had entered France and were moving to surround Paris. They reached the outskirts of the city on June 29, and Napoleon fled to Rochefort on the Southwestern coast of France when he heard the Prussians intended to capture him dead or alive. In Rochefort he attempted to gain passage to the United States, but British ships were blocking every port. He finally demanded asylum from the British Captain Fredrick Maitland on the HMS Bellerophon on July 15, 1815.

Chapter 8:
Death and Legacy

Exile on St. Helena

Napoleon had requested asylum in London, but the British denied this request, and instead sent him to St. Helena, a small, remote island in the south Atlantic Ocean over 1,100 miles off the coast of Africa. The British did not want to risk his return again. He was imprisoned in a house on the island that had been converted from a horse stable. He had a small cadre of followers with him, but was guarded at all times by 2,000 soldiers and 2 ships that circled the island 24 hours a day. He was endlessly bored, and completely defeated. He said, "To die is nothing, but to live defeated without glory is to die every day."

He ranted to his compatriots about the state of the world, and explained why he had lost various battles, particularly Waterloo. Finally, he decided to produce his memoirs, which he dictated to his secretary day after day. His memoir became his opportunity for a final victory. He discussed his decisions, his victories, and his losses, giving everything an aura of legend that carried his name into the future, and ensured his place in history. He recalled his greatest battles: the Pyramids, Murango, and Austerlitz. "These are granite," he said. "The tooth of envy is powerless there."

Aside from his military victories, Napoleon had established many institutions that would remain for centuries. His Civil Code, the Bank of France, his bridges over the River Seine, the system of secondary schools he created, and the many other roads, canals, and libraries he built during his reign. In his memoir, he called himself the savior of the revolution, and claimed he wanted peace. He insisted that the kings of Europe were opposed to the modern man, embodied by him and his attempt to spread the revolution to the rest of Europe. His memoirs were extremely successful, and helped to create a lasting image of Napoleon as a man of genius and determination. His life, therefore, is usually viewed somewhere between hero and villain. "My downfall raises me to infinite heights," he said. "If Christ hadn't been crucified he would never have been God."

Though he had been a tyrant and had led over 3 million soldiers to their deaths, his book cast him as a martyr, and he gained many followers over the years. He was able to write his one history, and in this way challenge the common notion that history is written by the victorious. The Arc de Triomphe stands in Paris today, commissioned by Napoleon in 1806, to honor those soldiers killed in the

French Revolution and Napoleon's Wars. In February 1821, after five years on St. Helena, Napoleon's health began to decline. He made peace with the Catholic Church, and died on May 5, 1821 after confession. His last words were, "France, army, head of the army, Josephine."

He was denied his wish to be buried on the banks of the Siene by the British governor, who ordered him buried on the island. In 1840, his remains were obtained by King Louis Philippe, who gave Napoleon a state funeral on December 15, 1840. His body was processed under the Arc de Triomphe, and eventually entombed in a crypt under the dome at Les Invalides.

Epilogue

"It is the cause, not the death, that makes the martyr."

—**Napoleon Bonaparte**

Napoleon's reign over the French Empire brought in a new age of warfare to Europe. Never before did hundreds of thousands of troops meet in single battles to decide the shape and future of nations. During his reign, his implementation of the Civil Code in France and throughout the French Empire helped to create a new legal system that still stands in Europe today, and also influence many other legal systems around the world. His struggles in the name of equality and freedom weakened the power of the monarchs of Europe. His ambitions and his belief in himself as something divine—or at least inspired by the divine—eventually led to miscalculations on the field of battle, but it still took all of Europe rising up at once to defeat him.

By the time of his final exile, he had motivated millions of soldiers to follow him into battle with the idea to bring honor to themselves and their Emperor, and glory to France. In his exile, he wrote his own history in his favor, and painted himself as a martyr of the Revolution. He came to be known for the many great things he achieved: his Civil Code, his expedition to Egypt, and the many public works he brought to France. He also pointed out his faults: his tyrannical rule, his loss in Russia, and his callous regard for the millions who were killed in service of his glory. In the context of history, his rule was not unlike that of many other kings, but the ideology and propaganda he used to secure popular support for his Empire drew an entire nation under his will. For his influence on history he will always be remembered, and because of this he must be respected.

Sources

Gengembre, Gérard, Pierre Jean. Chalenc̦on, and David Chanteranne. Napoleon: The Immortal Emperor. New York: Vendome, 2003. Print.

Roberts, A. Napoleon: A Life. Penguin Group, 2014

Philip Dwyer, Napoleon (2008)

Chandler, David. The Campaigns of Napoleon. Scribner, 1966

Schom, Alan (1997). Napoleon Bonaparte. HarperCollins.

Bell, David (2007). The First Total War. Houghton Mifflin Harcourt.

McLynn, Frank (1998). Napoleon. Pimlico.

Made in the USA
San Bernardino, CA
04 June 2018